# Polish Desserts!

# Polish Cookie, Pastry and Cake Recipes

## Kathy E. Gary

© 2012 by Kathy E. Gary

ISBN-13: 978-1479110049
ISBN-10: 1479110043

All Rights Reserved. No part of this publication may be reproduced in any form or by any means, including scanning, photocopying, or otherwise without prior written permission of the copyright holder.

First Printing, 2012

Printed in the United States of America

**Disclaimer/Legal Notice**
The information presented represents the view of the author as of the day of publication. Due to the rate at which conditions change, the author reserves the right to alter and update her opinions based on new conditions.

This book is for informational purposes only. While every attempt was made to accurately state the information provided here, neither the author nor her affiliates or publisher assume any responsibility for errors, inaccuracies or omissions. Any slights to people or organizations are unintentional.

**Photo Credits**
*Thank you for sharing your amazing talent!*
Cover Photo taken by Magic Madzik
Kolacky picture taken by Eric Schmuttenmaer
Tart picture taken by Salim Fadhley
Babka picture taken by Kochtopf

# Polish Desserts!

# Polish Cookie, Pastry and Cake Recipes

## Dedication

This book is dedicated to my mother, a second generation Polish-American. Through her dedication and creativity, she passed down a love of Polish culture and cuisine. I will be forever grateful.

## Other Books by Kathy Gary

*Passionate About Pierogies*

*Going Donuts For Paczki*

*Brunching on Bialys, Blini and Blintzes*

*Easy and Delicious Fudge*

*Visit Kathy's blog: http://www.kathygary.com*

Polish Desserts!

## Table of Contents

**Introduction** ................................................. 7
**Polish Dessert Recipe Tips** ............................ 9
**Polish Cookie Recipes** ................................. 11
   Angel Wings/Chrusciki ................................. 13
   Aunt Mary's Chrust Recipe ........................... 15
   Baked Chrusciki ............................................ 17
   Pam's Jam Kolaczki ....................................... 18
   Sweet Cheese Kolaczki ................................. 20
   Lily's Lemon Cookies .................................... 22
   Cat-Eye Kocie Oczka ..................................... 24
   Perfect Pierniki ............................................. 25
**Polish Pastry Recipes** ................................. 27
   Mazurek Fingers ........................................... 27
   Great-Aunt Daisy's Date Rolls ...................... 30
   Christmas Eve Lamance ............................... 31
   Polish Nut Tarts ............................................ 33
   Aunt Sabina's Polish Style Apple Pie ........... 35
**Polish Cake Recipes** ................................... 37
   Honey of a Babka Cake ................................ 38
   Deliciously Simple Babka ............................. 40
   Uncle Dan's Polish Baba ............................... 41
   Grandma's Makowiec .................................... 43
   Kolacz Weselny – Traditional Polish Wedding Cake . 46
**Final Thoughts** ........................................... 49

# Polish Desserts!

# Introduction

Welcome to **Polish Desserts! Polish Cookie, Pastry and Cake Recipes!**

Thank you for picking up the 4th book in my Ethnic Foods series. Growing up surrounded by a grandmother and several great-aunts from Poland, the fragrance of good foods cooking was always in the air. Even when times were tough, my grandmother could make a feast on a shoestring budget.

Some of the happiest times in my memory are those times that I shared with my grandmother baking. Baking was an event around the holidays, especially Christmas and Easter. Now, with my own children and grandchildren, we often make these desserts throughout the year. Nothing makes me feel more "at home" than sharing a Babka with my family, and nothing says, "Welcome to the Neighborhood" like a plate of homemade Chrusciki.

Many desserts in this book take a little time to prepare, but they are quite worth the effort. Some may require a 'knack' to get the dessert to look perfect. With practice it will come. In the meantime, you and your family can savor every delicious bite regardless. And let's be clear: none of these desserts could be considered healthy by anyone's standards. But if you are able to indulge in a fabulous, higher calorie treat from time to time, the desserts in this book will definitely fit the bill!

I hope you enjoy this book, and making and eating the desserts within, as much as my family and I do!

Happy Cooking!

~ Kathy

## Polish Desserts!

# Polish Dessert Recipe Tips

**Vanilla Sugar.** Some of the following recipes call for vanilla sugar. This product can be purchased in gourmet grocery stores or online. You can also make your own.

To make vanilla sugar from vanilla extract, mix 1 teaspoon vanilla extract with 1 cup of granulated sugar. To make vanilla sugar with vanilla powder mix 1 teaspoon vanilla powder with 1 cup powdered sugar.

To make vanilla sugar with vanilla beans (this is my favorite way to make it as it has the best flavor), you will need one vanilla bean and 2 cups of sugar. Cut the vanilla bean open, lengthwise. Carefully remove the seeds by scraping the inside of the bean with the dull side of a knife. Mix with the sugar.

Store the vanilla sugar in an airtight container. Leave it for a week or so prior to using for best flavor. Once you have tasted vanilla sugar you may want to use it in many of your baked goods recipes. It is also delicious in coffee and tea!

**Frying Tools and Tips.** The following tools and tips can help making Polish baked goods a bit easier.

# Polish Desserts!

**Deep Fryer or Cast Iron Skillet.** Some of the Polish cookies can be either fried or baked. Frying is most common and if you choose to go that route, you will need a deep cast iron skillet that can safely hold about 2 inches of hot oil, or a deep fryer. When frying be extra careful as hot oil can spit. When cooking with children, I prefer to bake instead of fry as it is the safer option.

**Frying Thermometer.** For cookies that are fried, a frying thermometer can help to ensure that the cookies fry to an even consistency every time. A frying thermometer is essential to be able to monitor the temperature of the oil.

**Tongs.** For fried cookies, a good set of metal tongs is necessary to remove them from the oil after they have been cooked.

**Keeping Baked Goods Fresh.** Especially during times of high humidity, many baked goods become stale quickly. Keep all uneaten baked goods in an airtight container, or freeze until ready to use.

Polish Desserts!

# Polish Cookie Recipes

*"Think what a better world it would be if we all, the whole world, had cookies and milk about three o'clock every afternoon and then lay down on our blankets for a nap."* ~Robert Fulghum

By far my favorite of all of the Polish cookies my grandmother would make are Angel Wings. That is what

# Polish Desserts!

we called them as children, and what my children and grandchildren call them.

The Polish name is Chrusciki, Chrust or Faworki. These are light, flaky pastry dough that is cut into diamond shape, sliced in the middle and an end pulled through the cut. They resemble a bow tie, or angel wings. They are typically fried and then topped with powdered sugar. Quite simply, they melt in your mouth and it's almost impossible to eat only one!

When I was growing up Chrusciki were popular at weddings and holidays. They take some time to make, but I enjoy them so much I make them throughout the year. What follows are two different recipes for fried Chrusciki, one of which has rum. I have also included a recipe for baked Chrusciki, which is a slightly healthier option than frying and is a safer option if you are cooking with children.

Included in this section are also lemon cookies that are just so amazing that I often double the batch! Also spice cookies called pierniki and cookies filled with jam such as kolaczki (pictured above) and kocie oczka. If you have never had these cookies before, you are in for quite a treat!

*Polish Desserts!*

## Angel Wings/Chrusciki

Of the three chrusciki recipes here, this is my family's favorite. It is important to roll the dough out thin. That is what makes the cookie just melt in your mouth. Be careful when dealing with the hot oil as it may spatter. Chrusciki tend not to store well, so keep in an air-tight container and eat soon after making (within a day or two is best). If they become limp, you can place them in a 350 degree (F). oven for a few minutes and they will regain their crispiness.

**Ingredients**
5 large egg yolks
1 large whole egg
1/2 teaspoon salt
1/4 cup confectioners' sugar
1/4 cup heavy cream
1 teaspoon vanilla
1 tablespoon rum
2 cups all-purpose flour
Canola or vegetable oil
Confectioners' sugar

**Directions**
In a large bowl, combine the egg yolks, whole egg and salt. With an electric mixer, beat at high speed until thick and lemon colored. This should take about 5 minutes. Beat in sugar, cream, vanilla and rum. Slowly add the flour and beat about 5 minutes more.

Flour a surface and place the dough. Divide the dough in half and cover with plastic wrap or a towel. Set aside for 20 minutes.

Roll out one of the dough pieces to 1/8-inch thickness. Cut into 2-inch-wide strips about 4-inches long. I use a sharp knife but you can also use a pastry wheel.

## Polish Desserts!

In a large, deep skillet, heat about 2 inches of oil to 350 degrees (F). If you use a temperature gauge you will be able to keep the oil at a consistent temperature.

Make a slit lengthwise in the center of each strip of dough and pull one end through the slit to form a bow.

I fry 5 angel wings at a time (because that is what fits in my skillet) for 1 minute or less per side or until golden. It is important to watch closely as they cook as they fry quickly.

Remove angel wings with medal tongs and drain on paper towels.

When the angel wings have cooled, dust with confectioners' sugar.

## Makes 6 dozen.

*Polish Desserts!*

# Aunt Mary's Chrust Recipe

Chrusciki are also known by many as Chrust which means brushwood. It is a term used to describe the appearance of these tasty twist treats. This recipe has fewer ingredients and some prefer the lighter taste to the recipe above.

**Ingredients**
5 egg yolks
1/2 teaspoon salt
3 tablespoons sugar
3 tablespoons sour cream
2 1/2 cups flour
1 tablespoon vanilla
Vegetable oil for frying
Powdered sugar for dusting

**Directions**
In a large bowl, combine the salt to egg yolks and beat with an electric mixer until thick and lemon colored. To this mix, add sugar and vanilla and mix well. Slowly add the sour cream and flour alternately, mixing well each time.

On a floured surface, place the dough and knead it well. When it starts to blister, knead it for another minute. Cut the dough in half so that it is easier to work with.

Roll the dough very thinly, about 1/8-inch thickness and cut into strips about 4 inches long and two inches wide. I use a sharp knife but you can also use a pastry wheel. Continue until all of the dough has been used.

In a large skillet or deep fryer, preheat the vegetable oil to 350 degrees (F). If you use a temperature gauge you will be able to keep the oil at a consistent temperature.

## Polish Desserts!

With a sharp knife, make a 1-inch slit lengthwise in the center of each piece of dough and pull one of the ends through it.

Carefully drop each chrust in hot oil one at a time. Watch carefully as the dough cooks fast, less than one minute for each side. If using a skillet, turn them half way through.

When the dough turns a light brown, remove the chrust from the oil with metal tongs.

Place on paper towels to absorb oil and sprinkle with powdered sugar. Once cooled, store in an airtight container.

Makes 40-60 chrust depending on size.

*Polish Desserts!*

# Baked Chrusciki

This is a good recipe to use when children are helping, as there is no hot oil involved. Again, the thinner you can make the dough, the better these cookies are!

**Ingredients**
2 sticks of butter
8 oz. cream cheese, softened
2 1/2 cup of flour
1/2 teaspoon vanilla
2 eggs
confectioners' sugar to top

**Directions**
Preheat oven to 375 degrees (F).

In a large bowl, mix the butter, cream cheese, flour, vanilla and eggs with an electric mixer. Mix until all ingredients are mixed well.

On a floured surface, roll out the dough as thin as possible, about 1/8-inch thick.

With a sharp knife or pastry wheel, cut into rectangles, about 4-inches long and 2-inches wide.

With a sharp knife, cut a slit lengthwise in the center about 1-inch long. Pull one end through the slit.

Bake on an ungreased baking sheet at 375 degrees (F). for 12 minutes.

Sprinkle with powdered sugar once cooled. Makes about 50 chrusciki.

## Pam's Jam Kolaczki

My family makes kolaczki diamond-shaped, but I have also seen them round and square. They can be filled with cheese, jam, sesame seeds or nuts. I prefer kolaczki with raspberry jam, but I have also made them with sweet cheese, apricot and nuts. This cookie recipe is my sister's, which she altered from my grandmother's recipe. They are great to make ahead of time because you can freeze filled but unbaked kolaczki and then bake them frozen when you need them.

**Ingredients**
8 oz. cream cheese, softened
3 sticks butter, softened
3 cups all-purpose flour
2 (14-ounce) cans of fillings of choice (My family loves raspberry)
1/4 cup confectioners' sugar mixed with 1/4 cup granulated sugar (for dusting when rolling out the dough)
Confectioners' sugar to top

**Directions**
In a large mixing bowl with an electric mixer, mix cream cheese and butter until light and fluffy. Slowly add flour a little at a time and continue to mix well. Wrap dough in plastic and refrigerate for about an hour.

Heat oven to 350 degrees (F).

On a surface that has been sprinkled with equal parts of confectioners' sugar and granulated sugar, roll out the dough about 1/4-inch thick. (Do not use flour).

With a sharp knife, cut the dough into 2-inch squares.

With a spoon place about 1 teaspoon of filling in the center of each square. Overlap opposite corners of dough to the center over filling. This will create an oblong cookie. To make square cookies, overlap both opposite corners so that all four corners meet in the center encasing the filling.

Place the cookies on an ungreased baking sheet and bake for 15 minutes or until cookies begin to brown.

Remove from oven and from baking pan.

When the kolaczki have cooled completely dust with confectioners' sugar.

Store these cookies in an air-tight container.

Makes about 5 dozen cookies.

## Sweet Cheese Kolaczki

These kolaczki are sweet and delicious. We make these for all holidays!

### Cheese Filling Ingredients
8 oz. package of softened cream cheese
1 cup cottage cheese
1 egg yolk
1/2 teaspoon vanilla
1/4 cup sugar
1 tablespoon lemon juice
1/4 teaspoon nutmeg

### Cookie Ingredients
8 oz. package of softened cream cheese
1 cup (2 sticks) softened unsalted butter
2 cups all-purpose flour
1 cup confectioners' sugar (plus more for dusting cookies)
2 teaspoons baking powder

### Directions for Filling
In a medium-sized bowl, combine all of the filling ingredients. With an electric mixer, mix all of the ingredients until smooth, about 2 minutes. Set aside.

### Directions for Cookies
Preheat oven to 350 degrees (F).

Line cookie sheets with parchment paper and set aside.

In a large bowl with an electric mixer, beat cream cheese and butter for about one minute.

Sift flour, confectioners' sugar, and baking powder into another bowl.

## Polish Desserts!

Slowly add dry ingredients into cream cheese mixture, 1/2 cup at a time, beating while adding. Continue to beat for about two minutes after all of the dry ingredient mixture has been added.

With your hands, shape the dough into 3-inch size balls. Place them two inches apart on the lined cookie sheet. Press your thumb into each ball to make an indentation for the filling. Spoon about a teaspoon of filling into cookie.

Bake cookies in a 350 degree (F). oven for about 12 – 15 minutes, or until the bottom of the cookies are lightly brown. Remove from the oven and place the cookies on a wire rack to cool.

Dust with confectioners' sugar when the cookies have cooled.

Makes 30-40 cookies.

## Lily's Lemon Cookies

These cookies are light and melt in your mouth! The recipe was given to me by my good friend Lily whose own grandma from Poland used to make them for her. They are delicious with a cup of milk, coffee or tea. Although it is common to find similar cookies with an orange or tangerine filling, my family prefers lemon. Feel free to experiment!

**Ingredients for Cookie Dough**
2/3 cup superfine sugar
8 oz. softened butter
1 large lightly beaten egg yolk
2 teaspoons lemon juice
zest of 1 lemon (reserve 1/2 teaspoon for filling)
2 1/4 cups all-purpose flour

**Ingredients for Cookie Filling**
1/3 cup softened butter
4 cups confectioners' sugar
4 tablespoons lemon juice
1/2 teaspoon lemon zest
Milk as necessary
Confectioners' sugar to top

**Directions for the Cookie Dough**
Place the oven rack in the middle of the oven. Preheat oven to 375 degrees (F).

In a large bowl using an electric mixer, cream the superfine sugar and softened butter until light and fluffy. Beat in the egg yolk, lemon juice and half of the lemon zest. Slowly beat in the flour about 1/2 cup at a time until thoroughly mixed.

Drop a rounded spoonful of dough onto parchment-lined sheet pans, spacing the cookies about 2 inches apart. (I prefer to use a 1-inch cookie scooper so that the dough remains round).

Take a glass and dip the bottom into flour. Lightly press the dough to flatten it. Repeat with all of the dough balls, coating the bottom of the glass with flour as needed.

Bake for 8 to 10 minutes or until the edges begin to brown. Remove from oven and cool for about 5 minutes before transferring the cookies on to a wire rack to cool completely.

**Directions for Filling**
In a medium-sized bowl with an electric mixer, cream together the butter, confectioners' sugar, lemon juice and remaining lemon zest. If mixture is too thick, add milk 1 tablespoon at a time until the desired consistency is achieved. The filling should be thick but not like paste.

These cookies can be served sandwiched or not. To sandwich the cookies, place a dollop of filling on the flat side of one cookie using a teaspoon. Top with another cookie, flat side down. If you choose not to make sandwich cookies, just place a dollop of filling on the flat side of each cookie.

Dust the tops with confectioners' sugar.

## Makes 30-60 cookies depending on whether you sandwich them.

*Polish Desserts!*

## Cat-Eye Kocie Oczka

This cookie is one of my favorites! Kocie Oczka means "cat's eye" and the cookie has this name because it is a sandwich cookie that has jelly filling in the center, making it look like an eye. The filling can be apricot, raspberry or any type of jam that you prefer.

### Ingredients
3 cups all-purpose flour
2 sticks butter, cut into cubes
2 tablespoons vanilla sugar
1 cup sour cream
jam of choice (I like raspberry or apricot)
confectioners' sugar to top

### Directions
Preheat oven to 425 degrees (F).

Line baking sheets with parchment paper.

In a large bowl, cut butter into flour the way you might for pie dough. Add vanilla sugar and sour cream, and mix well with an electric mixer. Wrap dough in plastic and refrigerate for 2 hours.

On the baking sheet, roll the dough thinly and cut into 2-inch circles about 1/2-inch thick. Using a smaller, round cutter, cut the center out of half the circles. Reroll the scraps and cut more cookies.

Bake 10-12 minutes or until the cookies begin to turn brown.

Remove the baking sheet from the oven and when the cookies have cooled, spread a thin layer of jam on top of the whole cookies. Top with the cookies that have holes and sprinkle confectioners' sugar on top.

Store cookies in an air-tight container. Makes 30 cookies.

*Polish Desserts!*

# Perfect Pierniki

These spice cookies are excellent with a cup of tea on a cold winter's evening!

**Ingredients**
1 cup  honey
4 cups  flour
pinch of black pepper
1/2 teaspoon cinnamon
1/2 teaspoon nutmeg
1/2 teaspoon cloves
1/2 teaspoon allspice
4 eggs
1 cup  sugar
1 teaspoon baking soda, dissolved in a little water
butter – to grease baking pan

**Directions**
Preheat oven to 350 degrees (F).

Grease baking pans with butter.

In a small pan, over medium heat, while stirring, heat the honey until it boils. Remove from heat and allow it to cool to just warm.

In a large bowl, sift the flour with the spices.

In another large bowl, with an electric mixer, beat the eggs with the sugar until thick. Add the baking soda/water mixture, the honey, and the flour. Mix well.

On a floured surface, place the dough and roll it out to about 1/4-inch thickness. Using cookie cutters of your choice, cut out the cookies.

Place the cookies on the buttered baking sheet and bake at 350 degrees (F). for 10-12 minutes or until light brown.

The cookies can be eaten as is, or can be topped with a thin glaze of confectioners' sugar, water and vanilla extract.

# Polish Pastry Recipes

## Mazurek Fingers

I prefer this dessert cut into "fingers" for ease of eating. But it can also be served as a traditional cake, and sliced as such.

**Ingredients for Fingers**
3 eggs, separated
1/2 cup fine sugar
1/2 cup all purpose flour
1/2 pound semi sweet chocolate, coarsely grated
1 cup ground almonds

## Polish Desserts!

**Ingredients for Decoration**
1 1/3 cup red currant jelly
2/3 cup semi sweet chocolate, broken into pieces
1/4 cup unsalted butter

**Directions**
Preheat the oven to 400 degrees (F).

Line and grease a 11" x 7" pan.

In a large bowl, cream the egg yolks and sugar until pale yellow and thick. Slowly fold in the flour a little at a time.

In a small bowl, whisk the egg whites until stiff and fold them into the flour mixture.

Gently add the chocolate and almonds to the flour mixture.

Place the mixture into the tin and spread it out evenly.

Bake for 20-25 minutes at 400 degrees (F). until lightly browned.

Cool in the tin for 5 minutes and then turn out on to a wire rack to cool.

To decorate, warm the jelly in a bowl over hot water and spread over the mazurek.

Let it set completely and then chill for about 20 minutes.

In another bowl, over hot water, melt the chocolate and butter. Remove from the heat and let cool for just a few minutes so that the mixture does not thicken.

## Polish Desserts!

Pour the chocolate on top of the mazurek and spread it evenly.

Let it set completely before cutting the pastry into fingers.

## Great-Aunt Daisy's Date Rolls

These cookies are easy and fun for children to make as well!

**Ingredients**
1 cup of butter
1/2 lb. of cream cheese
2 cups of sifted flour
1/4 teaspoon of salt
confectioners' sugar
pitted dates

**Directions**
Preheat oven to 375 degrees (F).

In a large bowl, cream the butter and cream cheese together. Slowly blend in the flour and salt.

Place the dough in the refrigerator and chill for several hours.

Sprinkle surface with powdered sugar. Roll the dough to 1/4 inch thickness and with a sharp knife or pastry wheel cut into strips that are 1-inch wide and 3-inches long.

Place a date in the center of each strip and roll the dough up.

Place the date roll-up folded side down on a cookie sheet.

Bake at 375 degrees (F). for 12-15 minutes or until the roll-up is light brown. Remove from the oven and allow to cool.

Once the pastries have cooled, sprinkle with powdered sugar. Makes 30-40 pastries.

*Polish Desserts!*

# Christmas Eve Lamance

When I was growing up, we would have Lamance every Christmas Eve. I think having this dessert only once a year made it all the more delicious!

**Ingredients for Pastry**
1 1/2 cups all-purpose flour
2 tablespoons butter
pinch of confectioners' sugar
1 egg yolk
3 tablespoons sour cream

**Ingredients for Dip**
2/3 cup poppy seeds, ground twice
1/4 cup ground almonds
2 tablespoons honey
1 ¼ cups sour cream

**Directions for Pastry**
Lightly grease baking sheets.

In a large bowl, sift the flour and cut in the butter. Stir in the sugar, egg yolk and sour cream. Mix until a soft dough forms.

Cut the dough in half and wrap each half in plastic wrap. Place in the refrigerator for about 15 minutes.

Preheat oven to 350 degrees (F).

Roll out the dough about 1/4-inch thin. Cut into squares and then in half to make triangles. Continue until all of the dough has been used.

Place the pastry on the baking sheets and bake for about 8-10 minutes or until golden brown. Remove from oven and cool pastry on wire racks.

**Directions for Dip**
Mix all of the ingredients together and then add 4 or 5 crushed pastries into the mixture as well. Mix well. Place dip in a small bowl and place pastries on a plate around the bowl for dipping.

Makes approximately 60 pastries.

# Polish Nut Tarts

**Ingredients for Tart Shell**
3/4 cup butter
2 3/4 cups all-purpose flour
2/3 cup confectioners' sugar
4 egg yolk
1 teaspoon vanilla

**Ingredients for Filling**
3 eggs, separate
handful of walnuts
1/2 cup jam (your choice)

**Directions for Tart Shells**
Preheat oven to 400 degrees (F).

In a large bowl, combine the butter, flour, confectioners' sugar, egg yolks and vanilla. Mix well.

On a floured surface, roll out the dough about 1/4 inch thick.

With a cookie cutter or a floured upside down glass, cut out circles to fit into individual tart pans.

Place tart pans with the dough into oven and bake for 8-10 minutes or until golden. Remove from oven and cool.

Reduce oven to 325 degrees (F).

**Directions for Filling**
In a small bowl, beat egg yolks, sugar and vanilla for about 5 minutes.

## Polish Desserts!

In another small bowl, beat the egg whites until they become stiff. Fold in the walnuts and mix gently.

Spread about 1/2 teaspoon of jam on the bottom of each tart and then top with the filling mixture.

Place tarts back into the over and bake for another 10-12 minutes at 325 degrees (F).

Makes 2 dozen tarts.

*Polish Desserts!*

# Aunt Sabina's Polish Style Apple Pie

## Ingredients for the Filling
8-10 baking apples, peeled and cored, cut into cubes
1 tablespoons lemon juice
2 tablespoons sugar
1 teaspoon vanilla

## Ingredients for the Pastry
1 1/2 cups all purpose flour
3/4 cup butter, chopped
1/2 cup light brown sugar
1/2 teaspoon salt
3 egg yolks
2 tablespoons sour cream

## Directions for Filling
In a bowl toss the chopped apples with the lemon juice.

In a large skillet, over medium-high heat, cook the apples for about 10 minutes until apples are soft. Remove from heat and set aside.

## Directions for the Pastry
Preheat oven to 350 degrees (F).

Lightly butter an 8" round cake pan.

In a large bowl, combine the flour and butter. Mix together until it has the consistency of bread crumbs. Mix in the sugar and salt. Add the egg yolks and sour cream. Mix until dough-like. Refrigerate for about an hour.

Using about 2/3 of the pastry dough, roll it out into a circle. Using this dough, cover the bottom and sides of the pan. Fork the pastry shell and prebake it for 12 minutes in 350 degree (F) oven. Remove from oven and let cool.

Roll the remaining pastry about 1/4-inch thick and cut it into stripes about 1/2 wide using a knife or pastry wheel.

Spread the apples evenly through the pastry shell. Place the pastry strips on top of the apples parallel to each other, so that there is little space in between each strip.

Bake the pie for about 25-30 min, till the top is golden brown. Remove from the oven and let cool. Then it easily cuts into nice pretty pieces.

This dessert is delicious as is, or served with vanilla ice-cream.

Makes 6-8 servings.

# Polish Cake Recipes

The following recipes are some of my family's favorites. Traditionally Babka is a single large ring-shaped cake filled with candied fruit, or a braided cake filled with cinnamon or in modern times, chocolate.

Listed here are the recipes for two different versions of Babka that we really enjoy. Also included is a recipe for Baba, which is a smaller cake and was traditionally served at Easter with a small lamb molded from sugar placed in the center.

Next is a recipe for Makowiec, which is similar to a poppy seed cake. And finally is a recipe for kolacz weselny, also known as a Polish wheel cake. Traditionally it was served at Polish weddings. Although this recipe is a considerable amount of work, it is worth it.

# Honey of a Babka Cake

**Ingredients**
3 large eggs
1 tablespoon fresh lemon juice
grated rind of 1 lemon
1/3 cup vegetable oil or olive oil
1 cup honey
1 cup warm black coffee
3 1/2 cups all-purpose flour, sifted
2 1/2 teaspoons baking powder
1 teaspoon baking soda
1/2 teaspoon salt
1/4 teaspoon cream of tartar
1 cup sugar
1 teaspoon cinnamon
1/2 cup slivered almonds

**Directions**
Preheat the oven to 350 degrees (F).

Grease and flour a 10-inch tube pan.

## Polish Desserts!

In a large bowl, with an electric mix, combine and mix the eggs, lemon juice, lemon rind, oil, honey and coffee. Continue to mix on low speed until blended.

Slowly add the flour, baking powder, baking soda, salt, cream of tartar, sugar and cinnamon. Continue to mix for 4-5 minutes or until well blended.

Mix in the almonds.

Spread the batter into prepared tube pan.

Bake in the oven for 45-50 minutes. Toothpick inserted in the center of the cake should come out clean.

Makes 12 servings.

## Deliciously Simple Babka

This is a simple recipe that creates a cake similar to sponge cake. You can also add dried fruit and/or candied peel if you'd like.

### Ingredients
1/4 cup butter
1 cup confectioners' sugar
1 teaspoon vanilla extract
3 eggs, separated
1/4 cup milk
1 1/2 cups flour
1 teaspoon baking powder
confectioners' sugar to top

### Directions
Preheat the over to 350 degrees (F).

Grease and flour a 7 1/2 x 4 1/2-inch loaf tin.

In a large bowl, beat the butter in a bowl until soft. Gradually mix in the confectioners' sugar.

Stir in the vanilla and egg yolks. Slowly add the milk, mixing in small spoonfuls of flour. This will keep the mixture from curdling.

Sift the remaining flour with the baking powder and stir it into the mixture.

Whisk the egg whites until stiff and fold it into the mixture. Place the mixture into the prepared loaf tin.

Bake for 40-45 minutes, until the cake has risen and is a golden brown. Turn out the babka on a wire rack to cool.

Dust with confectioners' sugar when cool.

Makes 10-12 servings.

## Uncle Dan's Polish Baba

### Ingredients
3 teaspoons dried yeast
1/2 cup warm milk
1 cup confectioners' sugar
4 cups wheat flour
2/3 cup raisins
1/3 cup chopped candied peel
1 cup blanched almonds, chopped
2 eggs, beaten
4 egg yolks
1/2 cup butter, melted
confectioners' sugar to dust

### Directions
In a cup, place the warm milk and 1 teaspoon of confectioners' sugar and stir. Add the dried yeast. Leave the yeast mixture in a warm place until foamy.

In a large bowl, sift the flour and mix in the fruit and nuts with the remaining confectioners' sugar. Make a well in the middle, and add the eggs, yolks, melted butter and yeast liquid.

Mix the remaining dry ingredients into the liquid to make a very soft dough. Mix this with your hand until elastic and smooth. Cover and let rise in a warm place until doubled in size. This should take about 2 hours.

Grease a Bundt pan.

Punch down the dough with your hand, then place it in the Bundt pan and press it down well. Cover loosely with cling wrap or towel and place in a warm place until the dough has risen to the top of the pan, about another hour.

## Polish Desserts!

Preheat oven to 350 degrees (F).

Bake the baba for about 40-45 minutes, or until it is golden brown.

Leave in the pan for about 5 minutes then turn out on a wire rack to cool.

Dust with confectioners' sugar when cool.

Makes 12 servings.

*Polish Desserts!*

# Grandma's Makowiec

My grandmother would serve this dessert often with tea. I have altered the dough from her original recipe to include the sour cream and powdered sugar. I find it adds a moister texture and sweeter dough.

## Ingredients for Filling

1 lb. poppy seeds
3/4 cup sugar
1 teaspoon vanilla extract
2 tablespoons butter
1 egg
1/4 cup honey
1/4 cup candied orange peel
1 teaspoon grated lemon rind
1/4 cup chopped walnuts
1/4 cup chopped almonds
1/2 cup golden raisins
2 egg whites

## Ingredients for Dough

1 tablespoon instant yeast
1/4 cup warm water
4 1/2 cups all-purpose flour
3/4 cup butter
2 eggs
2 egg yolks
1/2 cup sour cream
1 cup powdered sugar
1 teaspoon vanilla extract
1/2 teaspoon salt
2 teaspoons grated lemon peel

## Ingredients for Glaze

1 cup powdered sugar
1 tablespoon lemon juice
2 tablespoons boiling water

## Directions for Filling:

In a medium-sized saucepan, place the poppy seeds and cover with water. Bring to boil and then remove from heat and let stand until cool. When the poppy seeds have cooled, strain them through a fine strainer.

In a blender, grind the poppy seeds, walnuts, and almonds.

In a skillet over low heat, melt the butter. Add the poppy seed mixture and sugar and continue to simmer over low heat for about 2 minutes.

Stir in the egg, honey, orange peel, lemon peel, and raisins. Remove from heat.

Whip the egg whites until stiff and gently add to the poppy seed mixture. Let cool.

## Directions for Dough

Place the yeast in the warm water.

Cut the butter into the flour and combine until the texture is similar to bread crumbs. Mix in the salt and sugar.

Mix in the yeast, eggs, egg yolks, sour cream, vanilla extract, and lemon rind until thoroughly mixed.

With the dough, form a ball and place on floured surface. Knead the dough for 8-10 minutes until the dough is smooth.

Divide the dough in two. Roll out each piece about 1/4-inch thin to a square-ish shape.

# Polish Desserts!

Spread half of the filling onto each piece and then roll the dough. Seal the seam and place the rolled dough onto a baking sheet, seam side down.

Cover with a damp towel and set aside to rise for 80-90 minutes.

Bake in a 350 degree (F) oven for 30-35 minutes, or until the exterior is golden brown. Allow to cool.

In a small bowl, with a spoon mix the powdered sugar, lemon juice and hot water to create the glaze. Dribble glaze over the poppy seed roll when the roll has cooled.

Each roll makes 8 servings.

# Kolacz Weselny – Traditional Polish Wedding Cake

This cake was traditionally served at weddings. It is so good you will want to make it often! It is a bit of work, but it is very much worth it!

**Ingredients for Cheese Filling**
4 cups dry cottage cheese or farmer's cheese
4 egg yolks
2 cups granulated sugar
1 tablespoon vanilla sugar

**Ingredients for Cake**
2 tablespoons active dry yeast
1/4 cup warm water plus 1 tablespoon sugar
3/4 cup granulated sugar
1/2 cup unsalted butter
2 eggs
2 cups warm milk
4 1/2 cups all-purpose flour
pinch of salt
milk to brush

**Directions for Cheese Filling**
In a blender, blend the cheese for just a few seconds until smooth.

In a large bowl with an electric mixer, mix egg yolks, sugar and vanilla sugar. Beat until pale yellow and creamy, 8-10 minutes. Add the cheese, a little at a time and continue to beat until smooth. Set aside.

**Directions for Cake**
In a small bowl, dissolve yeast and 1 tablespoon of sugar in 1/4 cup warm water. Let stand 5 to 10 minutes until foamy.

# Polish Desserts!

In a large bowl, mix sugar, butter and eggs. Add yeast mixture, 2 cups of milk, 2 cups flour and salt. Mix until well blended.

Stir in remaining flour a little at a time until dough is soft.

Place the dough on a floured surface and knead dough until smooth and elastic. Place the dough in greased bowl rotating the dough to coat all sides.

Cover the bowl with a clean damp cloth and let rise in a warm place until it doubles in bulk – about 1 1/2 to 2 hours.

Preheat oven to 350 (F).

Grease the sides and bottom of a 10-inch spring form pan.

Divide dough into thirds. Using your hands, gently press 1/3 of dough evenly over bottom and side of pan. Evenly spread cheese filling over the dough-lined pan.

On a lightly floured surface, roll out another 1/3 of dough to a 10-inch circle.

Place this dough circle over the cheese filling.

Using a pastry brush, lightly brush milk over top of dough.

Cut the remaining 1/3 dough in 3 even pieces. Roll 3 pieces into long ropes. Braid the ropes and place them around the outer edge of cake.

Lightly brush with milk.

Bake 50 minutes or until golden brown.

Cool cake in pan for 5 minutes and then remove from pan and cool completely on a rack. Makes 12 servings.

# Polish Desserts!

# Final Thoughts

Homemade Polish treats are exactly that – a treat! Whether you make them occasionally or for holidays or more often creating your own special days, Polish desserts are sure to bring a smile to everyone!

I enjoy passing down these recipes and traditions to my family and I hope that this book will encourage you to create your own family traditions. Remember that if you have children in your life, they love helping! It is a terrific way to create memories and develop some fine family chefs and bakers!

Wishing you happy creating, cooking and eating!

~ Kathy

Printed in Great Britain
by Amazon.co.uk, Ltd.,
Marston Gate.